GETTING Contrary out of Mary

GO GIRL SERIES

By Susan Sherwood Parr

WORD PRODUCTIONS

GETTING Contrary out of Mary

Word Productions LLC
Albuquerque, NM 87192 USA

The Go Girl Series:
Getting Contrary Out of Mary
by Susan Sherwood Parr

Back cover photo:
Mike Trompak: TIMELESS IMAGES PHOTOGRAPHY
www.timelessimagesphotography.net

Printed in the United States of America.

Library of Congress Catalog Card Number Pending
ISBN 978-0-9827998-1-9

Special Thanks...

To Nathan Moses...

For his contribution to help us learn to watch our attitudes and our bodies nutritional needs. Nathan, thanks for taking the time!

Contents

CHAPTER ONE

Get A Grip?

CLOSE THE LIPS

Mary, Mary quite contrary, how does your garden grow?

> *So why do you worry about clothing? Consider the lilies of the field, how they grow: they neither toil nor spin; and yet I say to you that even Solomon in all his glory was not arrayed like one of these.* (Matthew 6:24)

Did you ever wish you could just stop talking negatively, or change your negative thinking? Have you noticed that you are complaining about too many things? Have you noticed any of these things about yourself. It's easy to notice things about others. What is not as easy is to take a look at your own behavior.

You can be different. You can Change. "I can change."

This is NOT...

...a name-it claim-it solution;

...a formula;

...instantaneous;

...something you "can't have."

It if is NOT the above...what is it then? Through God's grace and His Word *you and I can experience real change...*

Contrary—Dictionary Definition:
Adjective |ˈkänˌtre(ˌ)rˌ|

1 opposite in nature, direction, or meaning : he ignored contrary advice and agreed on the deal. See note at opposite .
• (of two or more statements, beliefs, etc.) opposed to one another : his mother had given him contrary messages.
• (of a wind) blowing in the opposite direction to one's course; unfavorable.
• Logic (of two propositions) so related that one or neither but not both must be true. Compare with contradictory.

IN this book we will be praying about things such as our attitudes of heart and our speech. We want to stop being contrary, grumpy, unkind to others and:

...rest in who God IS
...rest in His Integrity
...rest in His promises in the Word of God

All in healing that takes place in our lives is through God's Word and grace. It is even through God's grace that we can be educated and made aware of natural things [such as nutrition] that can have an affect on us.

ME? Always Nice?
I hate to admit it, but I better: I have not always had the right attitude, I have not always been "sweet," and I have not always said the right things.

Ever Been Nasty, Grouchy, or Mean?

At times, life brings us either the unpleasant, or an unpleasant person, and we might not be the sweetest communicator around. OR...we might have been that person.

Oh, I'm not saying we ARE nasty or mean. NO! I think frequently we are more subtle than that. Oh we can be sneaky. Just the right jab, just the right insinuation. What on earth has happened to us? What has happened? You could be someone who relates to this all the time. That's okay; God is bigger.

There is hope for you and me. Hey, think of it this way...you've discovered it! We can fall into the Contrary Rut AND out of the Contrary Rut.

The Contrary Rut

I have a few questions for you. Let's locate what you think about this topic:

What do you do when you don't know what to do about your own conversation?

What do you do when you don't know what to do about your own thinking?

What do you do when you've lost control of your mouth?

What do you do when you just feel bad and things just don't seem to turn out right?

The above list of questions is exactly what this book is about. We can become better for praying about these parts of our personalities. We can become better in Christ for newly applying the principles God has already provided for us.

It's NOT Hard

The first thing you need to do is stop for a moment. I'm not telling you to "shut up" or "stop thinking." No. But I am telling you to stop long enough to consider how you have been and how you would like to be.

Lets Consider a Few Things"

Consider your Conversation
Consider your attitude
Consider what you think may be the reason
Consider where the words are coming from
Consider where the thinking is coming from

I am assuming that those reading this book are already born again in Christ into God's family. If you are not, pray the prayer and look at the scriptural reasons in the last chapter of this book, and then come back HERE.

Together we will go to the Father in Jesus' name to help you to pray about things—We will pray about this; pray about our attitudes and how we talk to people.

In some of my other books I mention a study done by Dr. Frederick Luskin at Stanford Medical on Forgiveness [a key to healing]. It is really an interesting study. It is the back of this book in a resource chapter on forgiveness with the various other important studies on it.

Needless to Say?

Needless to say...forgive anyone of anything you can think of. Ask God's help to do it, but get forgiveness in your heart. That is crucial!

The Soap Opera
- I am contrary
- I have tried everything and I still think that way.
- I am unable to say nice things to certain people.
- Is there something I need to clear up in my heart?
- Is there anything between me and God?
- Is there anything between me and someone else?

What Do I Want to Pray About?

_____

_____

_____

_____

_____

Take Action
1. Stop looking to yourself for the solution
2. Stop blaming anyone else for your words or heart.
3. No matter what the case is or was, God can help.
4. Read and think about the following Scriptures on words:

Our Words and Our Tongue
God's Word is life and reading and thinking about the Scriptures will change your life. Below are some verses geared toward the subject of our study...our words and what kind of words they are. So do it. Read them and think about them:

> _Even so the tongue is a little member and boasts great things, See how great a forest a little fire kindles! And the tongue is a fire, a word of iniquity. The tongue is so set among our members that it defiles the whole body, and sets on fire the course of nature; and it is set on fire by hell. For every kind of beast and bird, of reptile and_

creature of the sea, is tamed and has been tamed by mankind. But no man can tame the tongue. It is an unruly evil, full of deadly poison. With it we bless our God and Father, and with it we curse men, who have been made in the similitude of God. Out of the same mouth proceed blessing and cursing. My brethren, these things ought no to be so. (James 3:5-10)

A fool's voice is known by his many words. (Ecclesiastes 5:3)

But let your 'Yes' be 'Yes,' and your 'No,' mean 'No.' For whatever is more than these is from the evil one." (Matthew 5:37)

Death and life are in the power of the tongue, and those who love it will eat its fruit. (Proverbs 18:21)

That if you confess with your mouth the Lord Jesus and believe in your heart that God has raised Him from the dead, you will be saved. For with the heart one believes unto righteousness, and with the mouth confession is made unto salvation. (Romans 10:9-10)

...For out of the abundance of the heart the mouth speaks. (Matthew 12:34)

There is one who speaks like the piercings of a sword, but the tongue of the wise promotes health. (Proverbs 12:18)

Let no corrupt word proceed out of your mouth, but what is good for necessary edification, that it may impart grace to the hearers. (Ephesians 4:29)

Set a guard, O LORD, over my mouth; keep watch over the door of my lips. (Psalm 141:3)

A soft answer turns away wrath, but a harsh word stirs up anger. The tongue of the wise uses knowledge rightly, but the mouth of fools pours forth foolishness. The eyes of the LORD are in every place, keeping watch on the evil and the good. A wholesome tongue is a tree of life, but perverseness in it breaks the spirit. (Proverbs 15:1-4)

For by your words you will be justified, and by your words you will be condemned. (Matthew 12:37)

The Cure
The first step in about any solution is to do the Forgiveness Check. Do it:

1. *Confess* your sins and unforgiveness and bad attitudes If we confess our sins, He is faithful and just to forgive us our sins and to cleanse us from all unrighteousness (1 John 1:9)

2. *Accept God's forgiveness* and you are ready to walk in faith with a conscience void of offense toward God.

   Let us draw near with a true heart in full assurance of faith, having our hearts sprinkled from an evil conscience and our bodies washed with pure water. (Hebrews 10:22)

Dr. Caroline Leaf: Thought Life
Dr Caroline Leaf is a noted Christian doctor, author, and speaker who is a Neuro-Metacognitive thinking and learning specialist who says:

87% to 95% of the illnesses that plague us today are a direct result of our thought life. What we think about affects us physically and emotionally. It's an epidemic of toxic emotions.

The average person has over 30,000 thoughts a day. Through an uncontrolled thought life, we create the conditions for illness; we make ourselves sick! Research shows that fear, all on its own, triggers more than 1,400 known physical and chemical responses and activates more than 30 different hormones. There are INTELLECTUAL and MEDICAL reasons to FORGIVE! Toxic waste generated by toxic thoughts causes the following illnesses: diabetes, cancer, asthma, skin problems and allergies to name just a few. Consciously control your thought life and start to detox your brain![1]

What Does the Bible Say About How we talk to people?
Provers 25:11 says "A word fitly spoken are like apples of gold in settings of silver." Don't you want to be the bearer of "Apples of Gold?"

Mary's Workbench

You're on the right path. You have decided to put God first and let Him change you in any way He desires.

What Is My Part?
1. Stop your bad words.
2. Remove all limits to what you think God can do.
3. Decide to change your words and thinking.
4. Enlarge your view of God.

What Is God's Part?
God cares for the lilies of the field and He cares for you (Luke 12). His promises are true and they belong to you (2 Corinthians 1:20). His Word is true (Rom. 3:4). God's Word will accomplish what it set out to do (Is. 55:11).

The Prayer

Dear heavenly Father, I ask You forgive me for my attitude. Forgive me for anything unkind I have ever spoken to anyone. Please change me. I cannot change my heart and words but you can. Please remove anything that is contrary out of my personality, In Jesus' Name. Amen

Promises to Cherish

"Behold, I am the LORD, the God of all flesh. Is there anything too hard for Me?" (Jeremiah 32:27)

For everyone who asks receives, and he who seeks finds, and to him who knocks it will be opened. (Matthew 7:8; Luke 11:10)

And my God shall supply all your need according to His riches in glory by Christ Jesus. (Philippians 4:19)

For all the promises of God in Him are Yes, and in Him Amen, to the glory of God through us. (2 Corinthians 1:20)

---

1. 1 Dr. Caroline Leaf, http://www.drleaf.net/thought-life

Today's Date_____

My Prayers

_____
_____
_____
_____
_____
_____
_____
_____
_____
_____
_____
_____
_____
_____
_____
_____
_____
_____
_____
_____
_____
_____
_____
_____
_____
_____
_____

Today's Date_____

My Answers

_____
_____
_____
_____
_____
_____
_____
_____
_____
_____
_____
_____
_____
_____
_____
_____
_____
_____
_____
_____
_____
_____
_____
_____
_____
_____
_____

Today's Date_____

My Thoughts

_____
_____
_____
_____
_____
_____
_____
_____
_____
_____
_____
_____
_____
_____
_____
_____
_____
_____
_____
_____
_____
_____
_____
_____
_____

CHAPTER TWO

Get class

TRASH THE SASS

So, you've discovered you're not always perfect in your choice of words. You and I will go to God with that. A little education in that area will never hurt you. Have you ever heard of the expression that suggests what you put in your body affects your health; what you expose yourself to affects your mind and life? Ever heard "Garbage in...garbage out?

Do you get what I am saying? Let's get some good input. We are like computers. Fill us with God's Word and we become Word-minded. Teach us about how to treat people; give us nice things to say; well, you get the drift.

Through God, His Word, and prayer we can change. He can change us. Learn some nice things to say.

Think about being kind to others. Care about what you might say to those around you. Touch someone else with those kind words. Your words that are truthful and encouraging can change a life.

Find someone who needs to be encoursged. That will definitely not be hard. We all need encouragement and people are all around you.

The Bible even says there is death and life in the power of the tongue. You have experienced how when someone encouraged you it changed your whole day.

The Soap Opera
• I have trouble thinking before speaking at times.
• It is a mystery to me—how can I change?
• At this point, I am willing for God's help!

What Do I Want to Pray About?

_____
_____
_____
_____
_____

Take Action
1.   Stop thinking about your needs for a moment.
2.   Decide you can replace what's negative in your with God's Word!
3.   Look at God's Word and decide you will be open to HIS work within you.
4. Change your attitude or ask God to change it.

Lose "McNasty"
- Look qway from your old habits or faults
- Look at God's Word.
- Look away from "me, me, me."
- Look to the Lord.

The Cure
- Realizing what I have been doing is a huge and good step in the right direction. You are no longer ignorant about it.
- You may be critical, contrary, unkind more than you realize. You may only get that way on occasion. There's nothing wrong with a personality makeover.
- Let's get better in Jesus Christ! Let's be recreated through His grace and the power of His Word.

Mary's Workbench

Now that you have realized you don't always speak with grace-filled words, you are on the right track. You can get better; you can grown in grace; God can make all things new again, and that's exciting!

What Is My Part?
1. Spend some time with the Lord.
2. When you run out of things to say, just sit quiety with Him.
3. Rest in Him.
4. Practice thinking of "nice" things to say to people?

Fifteen Nice Things to Say

1. I love you.
2. I'm on your side.
3. It's not the end...
4. I like you.
5. I'm glad to know you.
6. I'm praying for you.
7. I'm with you.
8. Have a great day.
9. I'm glad you are my friend.
10. I like spending time with you.
11. I'm here for you.
12. You're my best friend.
13. I respect you.
14. I respect what you think about things.
15. I hope everything works out!

What Is God's Part?

God will hear your prayer for kind words and healing in your attitude. That kind of prayer is definitely in His will. It has to do with removing sin from your life. That IS His will. He will help you. Give Him a try. He cares for you and me.

The Prayer

Dear heavenly Father, I ask You to forgive me for any unkind things that I have said to others. I have been selfish. I can't heal or help myself, and I ask for Your healing, grace, help, and comfort. Father, I also ask for grace to look out at others' needs to be able to reach out and help someone else. Your Word says if I ask anything according to Your will, You hear me and I have it (1 John 5:14). It also says that whatever I ask in Jesus name, you will give me (John 13:14). Father, I ask for all these things in Jesus' name. I rest my faith in Your integrity and in the integrity of Your holy Word (Numbers 23:19).

Think About It
Your doing the right thing to see change.

Promises to Cherish

If you then, being evil, know how to give good gifts to your children, how much more will your heavenly Father give the Holy Spirit to those who ask Him! (Luke 11:13)

For everyone who asks receives, and he who seeks finds, and to him who knocks it will be opened. (Matthew 7:8)

If you ask anything in My name, I will do it. (John 14:14)

Now this is the confidence that we have in Him, that if we ask anything according to His will, He hears us. And if we know that He hears us, whatever we ask, we know that we have the petitions that we have asked of Him. (1 John 5:14-15)

In all labor there is profit, But idle chatter leads only to poverty. (Proverbs 14:23)

Let no corrupt word proceed out of your mouth, but what is good for necessary edification, that it may impart grace to the hearers." (Ephesians 4:29)

"Set a guard, O LORD, over my mouth; keep watch over the door of my lips." (Psalm 141:3)

The eyes of the LORD are in every place, keeping watch on the evil and the good. A wholesome tongue is a tree of life, but perverseness in it breaks the spirit. (Proverbs 15:1-4)

"For by your words you will be justified, and by your words you will be condemned." (Matthew 12:37)

Today's Date_____

My Prayers

_____
_____
_____
_____
_____
_____
_____
_____
_____
_____
_____
_____
_____
_____
_____
_____
_____
_____
_____
_____
_____
_____
_____
_____
_____
_____

*Today's Date*_____

My Answers

_____
_____
_____
_____
_____
_____
_____
_____
_____
_____
_____
_____
_____
_____
_____
_____
_____
_____
_____
_____
_____
_____
_____
_____
_____

*Today's Date*_____

My Thoughts

_____
_____
_____
_____
_____
_____
_____
_____
_____
_____
_____
_____
_____
_____
_____
_____
_____
_____
_____
_____
_____

CHAPTER THREE

Get Vision

CONTRITION AND NUTRITION

Nathaniel Moses graduated from the University of New Mexico with a degree in Business Communications and Psychology. He began working in the family business, Moses Kountry Health Food Store [www.moseshealth.com], when he was 13 years of age. He now runs the business full time. He is actively involved in a local church and in ministry and has been a national televisioin guest on Sky Angel. I've asked Nathan for a bit of advice; and asked him if he would share a few tips that might help a contrary, grouchy, grumpy person.

What Does Nathan Moses Say?
Typically people are grouchy, grumpy because they have low blood sugar or are hypoglycemic.

Supplements that help support blood sugar:
Chromium/Vanadium; Cinnamon Extract (Cinnamon mimics insulin); Gymnema sylvestre; Nopal

Getting a good whole food multi-vitamin will help. The multi vitamins from the big box stores sometimes contain synthetic ingredients and are not recommended.

Some Other Advice

B Vitamins: The brain relies on nutrients to function properly. If your diet is not providing the essential nutrients, instability and mood swings can arise. B vitamins are particularly important for proper brain and neurological function. When B vitamin deficiencies arise, it can lead to unstable moods and depression. There are 3 B Vitamins that are particularly important for optimum brain function: vitamin B2 ribo-flavin, vitamin B3 niacin and vitamin B6. Food sources for the essential B vitamins include dark leafy green vegetables, meat, dairy, beans and grains. A complete B complex vitamin can be found at most health and supplement stores, or individual B vitamin supplements can be taken to achieve an optimum personal balance.

Zinc has a calming affect on the body and the brain. Deficiencies in zinc can cause agitation and mood swings. Zinc can be depleted by stress, which can aggravate anxiety. A balance of zinc and copper in the body is important for achieving and maintaining a stable mood. Zinc supplements are easily found in health food stores, but sometimes the nutrients obtained from foods are important. Foods high in zinc are oysters, egg yolk, meat, whole grains and split peas. According to the University of Maryland Medical Center, zinc is beneficial in small amounts. The recommended daily allowance consumed as a supplement is 8 to 11 mg a day. Zinc is essential but not a lot is needed. Mild zinc deficiencies are relatively common, but increasing zinc intake can benefit mood and brain function.

Magnesium, found in dark leafy greens, whole grains and nuts, is an important nutrient for physical and mental well being. Those suffering from depression and mood disorders many times also have a magnesium deficiency. Though magnesium deficiencies are rare, the effects can be noticeable and may include, insomnia, irritability and anxiety.

The Soap Opera
• I am tired of the whole thing and ready for change.
• I'm would be much happier if I learned to control my tongue.
• I could use a God-makeover AND a manners class.
• I am frustrated when I think about "what I am not."

What Do I Want to Pray About?

_____
_____
_____
_____
_____

Take Action
One: I'm going to get some class
Two: I'm going to stop the sass
Three: I'm going to trash my old ways
Four: I'm looking forward to what God can do.

The Cure
Look at the means; do what is apparent that you need to do.
Trust God to do a new work within you.
He will help you.
He CAN do it.
There is nothing to hard for Him.

Mary's Workbench

Just Do it! Do the Workshop.

What Is My Part?

1. Coffee break with Jesus or Time Alone with HIM is the key
2. Tell him of your troubles, fears, progress.
3. Look at your nutrition; make changes
3. Pray in detail about your personality; pray about your words
5. Pray [do the workshop] and thank God for what He is doing in your life.

What Is God's Part?

God will work in you to will and do of His good pleasure. He also says you are changed into the same image from glory to glory as by the Spirit of the Lord (see Promises to Cherish).

He knows full well that HE must do it. You can't. In fact, the best place to be to receive help is in a place of admitting to Him who and what you would be without that grace.

The Prayer

Dear God, I ask You to work in me to will and do of Your good pleasure. Create in me a clean heart and renew a right spirit within me. Make me holy, pure, and full of Your Holy Spirit. Change me in any way You want. Make me into what You want me to be. Help me step out of the the negative and unkindness that has been in my life. Help me be gracious, kind, encouraging, and whole; help me walk into the newness of life that You have for me, in Jesus' name.

Think About It
- God is great
- God cares about your life
- God will hear you and answer you

Promises to Cherish

Now to Him who is able to do exceedingly abundantly above all that we ask or think, according to the power that works in us, 21 to Him be glory in the church by Christ Jesus to all generations, forever and ever. Amen. (Ephesians 3:20)

But we all, with unveiled face, beholding as in a mirror the glory of the Lord, are being transformed into the same image from glory to glory, just as by the Spirit of the Lord (2 Corinthians 3:18).

In Him also we have obtained an inheritance, being predestined according to the purpose of Him who works all things according to the counsel of His will, that we who first trusted in Christ should be to the praise of His glory (Ephesians 1:11–12).

*Today's Date*_____

My Prayers

_____
_____
_____
_____
_____
_____
_____
_____
_____
_____
_____
_____
_____
_____
_____
_____
_____
_____
_____
_____
_____
_____
_____
_____
_____
_____

Today's Date_____

My Answers

_____
_____
_____
_____
_____
_____
_____
_____
_____
_____
_____
_____
_____
_____
_____
_____
_____
_____
_____
_____
_____
_____
_____
_____
_____

Today's Date_____

My Thoughts

_____
_____
_____
_____
_____
_____
_____
_____
_____
_____
_____
_____
_____
_____
_____
_____
_____
_____
_____
_____
_____
_____
_____
_____

CHAPTER FOUR

GiVe LoVe

GIVE APPLES

A word fitly spoken are like apples of gold in settings of silver. (Proverbs 25:11)

Don't you want to be the bearer of "Apples of Gold?" Well the verse below has to do with giving—we can give love, kindness, kind words, help in time of need:

Give, and it will be given to you: good measure, pressed down, shaken together, and running over will be put into your bosom. For with the same measure that you use, it will be measured back to you. (Luke 6:38)

Give the love of God to others.
Give His Word to others as often as possible.
Give kind and encouraging words to others.

The Soap Opera
- I've been unkind
- I've lacked sensitivity
- I have been selfish

What Do I Want to Pray About?

_____

_____

_____

_____

_____

Take Action
Take time to work on this; set some goals:

Goals You Can Set
1. Write a list of those in your life and thank those who are kind to you.

2. Write a list of ways to be good to your husband. Thank your husband for ways he helps you; for his work. Think of Ways to encourage him.

3. Write a list of things you can say or do for those close to you. Your goal will be to be kind or encourage everyone in your life in some way.

4. Make a list of those you have resented and write down any ideas of ways to be kind, things you can say, a card you can send.

5. Send an e-mail during the day just to say, "I love you" to your husband or others in your family.

You will begin to find that you will love people in a whole new way. When your mind is off of yourself and on others, a whole new world will open up to you. It will be a world of God, His Word, encouragement, kind words, and you will be happier for it!

The Cure

You are on the way to walking in Christ. A wonderful verse in god's word is "Christ in you the hope of glory..." Imagine. It says it is He who works IN us...what a marvelous freeing thought.

Mary's Workbench

Pray about every detail; God hears you. Get happy at the prospect of newness in your life. Now? Look forward to the limitless power of God in all of this. You're praying; you're hoping; you're trusting!

What Is My Part?

Be filled with His Word and surround yourself with a Word-atmosphere. Remember that a *Word-atmosphere* produces Holy Spirit fruit. John 6:63 clearly says that His Word IS Spirit and it is LIFE! The word "life" in the Greek, *zoe,* means *the essence of God.* Now that is exciting!

What Is God's Part?

God is working in your to will and do of His good pleasure. He never said you had to make yourself. He never said you must create a great personality...NO! God will always be with you. He will never leave you. He loves you.

The Prayer

Dear God, please lead and guide me in enlarge my vision of and what you can do in my life. Grant me the desire, wisdom, and grace to want to be an encourager and aperson who has good things to say to others. Please deliver me from all evil. Forgive me for all the unkind words and help those I have offended to forgive me. Thank you for what you are going to do, in Jesus' name. Amen.

Think About It

It is a good thing that you have agreed to pray about everything in your life. There's no better place for your needs to be than with the Lord. Spending time with Him each day is the number one priority to have help. Then, the time in God's Word is also critical. You can read it or listen to it. You can read long sections or promise books, but surrounding yourself with a Word atmosphere brings His life into your life!

Promises to Cherish

It is the Spirit who gives life; the flesh profits nothing. The words that I speak to you are spirit, and they are life. John 6:63

For this reason we also thank God without ceasing, because when you received the word of God which you heard from us, you welcomed it not as the word of men, but as it is in truth, the word of God, which also effectively works in you who believe. 1 Thessalonians 2:13

Therefore, my beloved, as you have always obeyed, not as in my presence only, but now much more in my absence, work out your own salvation with fear and trem-

bling; 13 for it is God who works in you both to will and to do for His good pleasure. Phil. 2:12-13

Now to Him who is able to do exceedingly abundantly above all that we ask or think, according to the power that works in us, 21 to Him be glory in the church by Christ Jesus to all generations, forever and ever. Amen. Ephesians 3:20-21

*Today's Date*_____

My Prayers

_____
_____
_____
_____
_____
_____
_____
_____
_____
_____
_____
_____
_____
_____
_____
_____
_____
_____
_____
_____
_____
_____
_____
_____
_____
_____

*Today's Date*_____

My Answers

_____
_____
_____
_____
_____
_____
_____
_____
_____
_____
_____
_____
_____
_____
_____
_____
_____
_____

*Today's Date*_____

My Thoughts

_____
_____
_____
_____
_____
_____
_____
_____
_____
_____
_____
_____
_____
_____
_____
_____
_____
_____
_____
_____
_____
_____
_____
_____
_____
_____

CHAPTER FIVE

Get the Keys

IT'S A BREEZE!

There are Four Keys to a Close Walk with God. Because they are so vital to life itself, I include them in all of my books. How can you leave out the keys, forgiveness, prayer, etc." You can't. These keys will help you know how to live, and how to make certain positive steps to change your direction.

One of the first most exciting Scriptures I heard as a new Christian said that God had foreordained steps for me to walk in. I couldn't believe it. ME? It was an awesome thought for me. Think about it. He has a plan for your life; He has a plan just for you.

The Soap Opera
- In myself I can do nothing.
- I'm realizing that I have sinned.
- I know God can help me.
- God can give me a new way of communicating

What Do I Want to Pray About?

_____

_____

_____

_____

_____

_____

Take Action

1. Refuse to worry about anything.

2. Pray in detail about everything.

3. Put Philippians 4:6–7 into practice.

4. Trust in God, His integrity, the integrity of His Word, and His promises.

The Cure

Resting and counting on God's integrity, the integrity of His Word and promises is the best thing you can do. Learning how to approach God and then seeing results is an exciting thing.

I _will_ receive God's grace for my words and attitude.

I will pray about my heart and words.

I will stand on the promises in the Bible.

I will thank Him for all He has done and is going to according to His will.

I can receive God's help after I pray.

Mary's Workbench

Don't get discouraged here. I know that God has heard and already began to answer your prayers. It is so wonderful to see His love working in your life! Keep faith in Him.

What Is My Part?
1. Key One: Put God and His Word first in your life.

2. Key Two: Find Christian friends; find healthy places to go and clean, fun things to do.

3. Key Three: Reassess your physical health. Your body are the temples of the Holy Spirit. Remember that you need proper nutrition and exercise.

4. Key Four: Get involved. This will rid you of that stagnant feeling. You will become spiritually healthy and happy when you get involved and give of yourself in some way.

Pray about these keys and these aspects of your life. Thank God and praise Him for what He is doing and is going to do in your life.

What Is God's Part?
God cares about every aspect of our lives and wants us to draw near to Him. He responds to our prayers.

1. The next time you spend time with the Lord, make it a point to sit quietly before Him. Give Him a chance to speak to you.

   Call to Me, and I will answer you, and show you great and mighty things, which you do not know. (Jeremiah 33:3)

In the day of my trouble I will call upon You, for You will answer me. (Psalm 86:7)

2. Remember—God hears you, loves you, and will answer you. It doesn't matter if at times you don't see answers immediately. God is at work!

As you do not know what is the way of the wind, or how the bones grow in the womb of her who is with child, so you do not know the works of God who makes everything. (Eccles.11:5)

The Prayer
Dear Lord, I want to be filled with your Holy Spirit. I want to pray about everything and I want you to move in my life in new ways. I want to love You more and feel loved by You. I pray for you to grant me continual grace. I want to do what is right and am happy that you can and will change me. Make me into what you want me to be. In Jesus name. Amen.

Think About it
• Do the Four Keys to a Close Walk with God.
• Put God first; follow the plan; enjoy peace with God, a hope, and a future.
• Live your life in praise and thanksgiving to God.

Promises to Cherish

Behold, I will do a new thing, now it shall spring forth; shall you not know it? I will even make a road in the wilderness and rivers in the desert. (Isaiah 43:19)

Behold, the former things have come to pass, and new things I declare; before they spring forth I tell you of them. (Isaiah 42:9)

Do not remember the former things, nor consider the things of old. (Isaiah 43:18)

Remember the former things of old, for I am God, and there is no other; I am God, and there is none like Me. (Isaiah 46:9)

I have declared the former things from the beginning; they went forth from My mouth, and I caused them to hear it. Suddenly I did them, and they came to pass. (Isaiah 48:3)

And God will wipe away every tear from their eyes; there shall be no more death, nor sorrow, nor crying. There shall be no more pain, for the former things have passed away. (Revelation 21:4)

I will bring the blind by a way they did not know; I will lead them in paths they have not known. I will make darkness light before them, and crooked places straight. These things I will do for them, and not forsake them. (Isaiah 42:16)

Today's Date_____

My Prayers

_____
_____
_____
_____
_____
_____
_____
_____
_____
_____
_____
_____
_____
_____
_____
_____
_____
_____
_____
_____
_____
_____
_____
_____
_____
_____

Today's Date _____

My Answers

_____
_____
_____
_____
_____
_____
_____
_____
_____
_____
_____
_____
_____
_____
_____
_____
_____
_____
_____
_____
_____
_____
_____
_____
_____

*Today's Date*_____

My Thoughts

_____
_____
_____
_____
_____
_____
_____
_____
_____
_____
_____
_____
_____
_____
_____
_____
_____
_____
_____
_____
_____
_____
_____

CHAPTER SIX

Get the Future

BYE BYE MARY

So look forward to what God can do in your life. You're on the way to newness and a creative God working in you to perfect that which concerns you. Here is what He promises::

And though the Lord gives you the bread of adversity and the water of affliction, yet your teachers will not be moved into a corner anymore, But your eyes shall see your teachers. Your ears shall hear a word behind you, saying, "This is the way, walk in it," Whenever you turn to the right hand Or whenever you turn to the left. (Is. 30:20-2)

I will lay waste the mountains and hills, and dry up all their vegetation; I will make the rivers coastlands, and I will dry up the pools. I will bring the blind by a way they did not know; I will lead them in paths they have not known. I will make darkness light before them, and crooked places straight. These things I will do for them, and not forsake them. (Is. 42:15-16)

And one more marvelous verse that confirms God's desire is to lead you and that He can actually lead you:

For if you live according to the flesh you will die; but if by the Spirit you put to death the deeds of the body, you will live. For as many as are led by the Spirit of God, these are sons of God. For you did not receive the spirit of bondage again to fear, but you received the Spirit of adoption by whom we cry out, "Abba, Father." Rom. 8:13-15

The Soap Opera
- I am not sure I can do this.
- I am concerned I will forget to pray.
- I hope I don't give up.
- I am scared.

What Do I Want to Pray About?

_____

_____

_____

_____

_____

Take Action
1. Pray each day. Spend that valuable time with Him.
2. Set a goal—one that is easy to accomplish.
3. Help someone this week.
4. Be encouraged. You're doing something!

The Cure
Remember that your words can hurt or help someone. Thank God you've chosen to let God move in your life. Thank God

He will move in your life. He is the cure. His Word is alive and working within you.

Mary's Workbench

What Is My Part?
Have some fun. You're already on the right track. Here are some things to do, that are easy for any of us:

Things To Do At Church
1. Become a part of a ministry at church.
2. Find people to listen to.
3. Children's ministry
4. Volunteer at the church office
5. Go to a Bible study.
9. Visit a Nursing Home.
10. Find a friend to meet with to share God's Word.

Things To Do In Everyday Life
A friend in Bible college once told me he was never lonely because he always made plans. Very interesting. I heard him that day. Part of my trouble was the lack of plans. Hence I would get very lonely. Get involved!

What Is God's Part?
God is true and His Word is true. He will never leave you or forsake you. He is more than enough. Men or women may lie, but God never lies. He is no respector of persons. That means: If He has done something for someone else, He will do it for you [according to His will].

The Prayer

Dear God, I am just going to thank you for the great and merciful God that you are. Thank you for coming into my life; thank you for remaining in my life and not giving up on me; thank you that I can come to you for new things and to change me. Take control of me all over again and make me into the kind of person you want me to be, in Jesus' name, amen.

Think About It

> *Do not remember the former things,*
> *Nor consider the things of old.*
> **Behold, I will do a new thing,**
> **Now it shall spring forth;**
> **Shall you not know it?**
> *I will even make a road in the wilderness*
> *And rivers in the desert.* Is. 43:18-19

What IS God's Will?

1. Salvation (Mark 16:16)

2. Forgiveness of sins (1 John 1:9)

3. Receiving God's grace (Romans 5:1–24)

4. Miracles and healing, according to His will (1 Corinthians 12:28)

5. Deliverance from evil—helping restore the damage caused by sins and circumstances (Jeremiah 3:22; Psalm 103:3; 107:20; Matthew 4:24; James 5:16)

6. Healing relationships where human will is open (Luke 4:18)

   God *can* do a new thing. He is not limited. This chapter will give you the keys you need to unlock the door to the new things God has for you. He is there for you. God loves you. Your relationship with God is your greatest gift. Nurture it. It will grow. All you are and can be comes from your life in Jesus Christ. Draw near to Him.

Walk with Him. Talk with Him. Philippians 4:19 says that God will provide all of your needs according to His riches in glory by Christ Jesus.

God takes care of us; He'll take care of you. I think that the most valuable blessings I have ever received have been those obtained because I lay on my face before God, entreating His forgiveness, love, mercy, and grace.

5. Deliverance from evil—helping restore the damage caused by sins and circumstances (Jeremiah 3:22; Psalm 103:3; 107:20; Matthew 4:24; James 5:16)

6. Healing relationships where human will is open (Luke 4:18)

God says, "Forget it!" What God is doing is in front of you. Think about that for a moment. Thirty seconds ago doesn't exist anymore. An unseen future is in front of you. What God can and will do is ahead of you. What does the Bible say about this?

Paul said:
"Not that I have already attained, or am already perfected; but I press on, that I may lay hold of that for which Christ Jesus has also laid hold of me. Brethren, I do not count myself to have apprehended; but one thing I do, forgetting those things which are behind and reaching forward to those things which are ahead, I press toward the goal for the prize of the upward call of God in Christ Jesus" (Philippians 3:12–14).

God Said:

*"I am the LORD, your Holy One, the Creator of Is-
rael, your King." Thus says the LORD, who makes a
way in the sea and a path through the mighty waters,
who brings forth the chariot and horse, the army and
the power (they shall lie down together, they shall not
rise; they are extinguished, they are quenched like a
wick): "Do not remember the former things, nor consider the things of old. Behold, I will do a new thing,
now it shall spring forth; shall you not know it? I will
even make a road in the wilderness and rivers in the
desert"* (Isaiah 43:15–19).

*Brethren, I do not count myself to have apprehended;
but one thing I do, forgetting those things which are
behind and reaching forward to those things which are
ahead, I press toward the goal for the prize of the upward call of God in Christ Jesus* (Philippians 3:13–14).

*So now, brethren, I commend you to God and to the
word of His grace, which is able to build you up and give
you an inheritance among all those who are sanctified*
(Acts 20:32).

Rise from Sleep; Rise from the Dead

Together we will work on these things. God is really alive—
Jesus has risen from the dead. You know, Lazarus' body had
begun to shut down and fully shut down. He died. His sisters
thought it was too late.

*Jesus said to her, "Did I not say to you that if you would
believe you would see the glory of God?" Then they
took away the stone from the place where the dead man*

was lying. And Jesus lifted up His eyes and said, "Father, I thank You that You have heard Me. And I know that You always hear Me, but because of the people who are standing by I said this, that they may believe that You sent Me." Now when He had said these things, He cried with a loud voice, "Lazarus, come forth!" And he who had died came out bound hand and foot with grave clothes, and his face was wrapped with a cloth. Jesus said to them, "Loose him, and let him go" (John 1:40–44)

Jesus can do anything in our lives. He is limitless. He can hope against hope give hope and life. I know this for myself. He is indeed the Resurrection and the Life, for you.

Leave yesterday behind you. It's not only a wonderful idea but it possible! God can give you a new beginning.

Promises to Cherish

Now this is the confidence that we have in Him, that if we ask anything according to His will, He hears us. And if we know that He hears us, whatever we ask, we know that we have the petitions that we have asked of Him (1 John 5:14–15).

Behold, the former things have come to pass, Now I declare new things; Before they spring forth I proclaim them to you. (Is. 42:9)

How will they preach unless they are sent? Just as it is written, "How beautiful are the feet of those who bring good news of good things!" (Rom. 10:15)

And He who sits on the throne said, "Behold, I am making all things new." And He said, "Write, for these words are faithful and true." (Rev. 21:5)

*Today's Date*_____

My Prayers

_____
_____
_____
_____
_____
_____
_____
_____
_____
_____
_____
_____
_____
_____
_____
_____
_____
_____
_____
_____
_____
_____
_____
_____
_____
_____

Today's Date_____

My Answers

_____
_____
_____
_____
_____
_____
_____
_____
_____
_____
_____
_____
_____
_____
_____
_____
_____
_____
_____
_____
_____
_____
_____
_____
_____

Today's Date_____

My Thoughts

_____
_____
_____
_____
_____
_____
_____
_____
_____
_____
_____
_____
_____
_____
_____
_____
_____
_____
_____
_____
_____
_____
_____
_____
_____
_____
_____
_____

Go Girl

TOOL KIT

CHAPTER SEVEN

Get the Annecdote

PRAYER & FORGIVENESS

In the back of this book there is a section of notes about forgiveness, and research from medical universities showing that healing can occur through forgiveness.

Forgiving others is powerful. Receiving forgiveness is also powerful. Think about having a clear conscience and the peace of mind that it brings. God can give this to us. Good advice: Forgive, and be forgiven.

Keys to Successful Prayer
This chapter will give you the keys to experiencing results in prayer. It's not a matter of using a key to "get want you want." There is no selfishness involved. I use the word "key" because I found, to my joy, that making a few changes in how I prayed totally regenerated my prayer life and filled my heart and mind with peace.

Be anxious for nothing, but in everything by prayer and supplication, with thanksgiving, let your requests be made known to God; and the peace of God, which surpasses all understanding, will guard your hearts and minds through Christ Jesus. (Phil. 4:6–7)

The above verse is the theme Scripture for the teaching on prayer. From the apostle Paul we get this advice: Don't worry; instead, pray about everything. It then adds that the peace of God, which surpasses understanding, will keep our hearts and minds through Christ Jesus |paraphrased|. What a promise! Of course, we must pray according to God's will and in line with what Scripture teaches us. But many things are God's will.

In the Old Testament, David prayed that God would overthrow and overturn the works of darkness, and in response God sent out His arrows and scattered the foe, lightnings in abundance, and He vanquished them (Psalm 18:14). There are many answers to personal prayers in the Bible. Have you ever wanted to pray but didn't know how to begin? Or have you tried everything but not received the joy and fulfillment you had hoped for in prayer?

Through these steps, you will become renewed in your excitement for spiritual things and about God Himself, His faithfulness, and the integrity of His Word.

The price Jesus paid for our sins at Calvary affords us the opportunity to be born again and to come into the family of God, which is the Christian's greatest gift. The relationship we can then have with our God is the next greatest gift.

Prayer is the key to building a close relationship with God. As you engage in prayer, you will never be the same again. Prayer need not be tedious. God does not require you to perform a list of prerequisites before He will answer you. Yet there are things that God asks of us.

Before You Start

Forgiveness Before you pray, you need to be sure there is nothing between you and God. You need to ask for forgiveness of your sins. You also need to forgive others of anything you have against them. How can we ask for forgiveness if we refuse to forgive others their trespasses against us (Luke 6:37 and 17:3)?

If I feel like I can't forgive, I ask for His help: "God, I can't forgive, but I ask You to love and forgive in and through me by Your Holy Spirit. Please give me the grace." This will work!

> *Leave your gift there before the altar, and go your way. First be reconciled to your brother, and then come and offer your gift.* (Matt. 5:24)

Studies on Forgiveness

Stanford Medicine, Volume 16, Number 4, Summer 1999, published a quarterly by Stanford University Medical Center: *The Art and Science of Forgiveness.* "If you feel good but want to feel even better, try forgiving someone." —FREDERIC LUSKIN, PH.D. You can research this on the Stanford Medical Website to read it in its entirety.

Receiving Forgiveness

Forgiving others is powerful, according to the above study, and it brings emotional and physical benefits to your life. It also can benefit the lives of those being forgiven. Perhaps there can now be the opportunity for healing in a once-severed relationship.

Forgiveness gives us a clear conscience and the associated peace of mind. "Forgive and be forgiven" is good advice. Let your requests be made known to God; and the peace of God, which surpasses all understanding, will guard your hearts and minds through Christ Jesus. Philippians 4:6–7

Mini Prayer Workshop

Let's Get Started!

1. Confess and receive forgiveness for any sin, including unforgiveness, doubt, unbelief, fear, and anything else that might be between you and God (1 John 1:9).

2. List your requests. "Let your requests be made known to God" (Philippians 4:6).

3. Take authority over the enemy. Pray that God will "overthrow and overturn the works of darkness" (2 Chronicles 25:8).

4. Pray in detail. Make specific (scriptural) requests to the Father in Jesus' name. You can always add "If it be Your will" to the end of a prayer if you don't know the will of God.

5. Place your trust in His specific promises. Know that we rest our faith in who God is, in His integrity, and in the integrity of His Word.

6. Thank God and praise Him for what He is doing according to His will. "By prayer and supplication with thanksgiving, let your requests be made known to God" (Philippians 4:6).

What Is GOD'S Part?

God is faithful. His promises are true (1 Corinthians 1:20). His Word is true (Romans 3:4). He will watch over His Word to perform it (Isaiah 55:11). So, when you find promises upon which to rest your faith, God is pleased. He will hear and answer you. You must realize that God has more love and understanding for His creation than we can possibly comprehend. He is also more powerful than we can grasp.

Promises to Cherish

Be anxious for nothing, but in everything by prayer and supplication, with thanksgiving, let your requests be made known to God; and the peace of God, which surpasses all understanding, will guard your hearts and minds through Christ Jesus. (Phil. 4:6–7)

Whatever you ask in My name, that I will do, that the Father may be glorified in the Son. If you ask anything in My name, I will do it. (John 14:13–14

Most assuredly, I say to you, whatever you ask the Father in My name He will give you. Until now you have asked nothing in My name. Ask, and you will receive, that your joy may be full. (John 16:23–24)

All the promises of God in Him are Yes, and in Him Amen, to the glory of God through us. (2 Corinthians 1:2)

Now to Him who is able to do exceedingly abundantly above all that we ask or think, according to the power that works in us, to Him be glory in the church by Christ Jesus to all generations, forever and ever. Amen. (Ephesians 3:20–21)

Today's Date_____

My Prayers

_____
_____
_____
_____
_____
_____
_____
_____
_____
_____
_____
_____
_____
_____
_____
_____
_____
_____
_____
_____
_____
_____
_____
_____
_____
_____
_____

Today's Date_____

My Answers

_____

_____

_____

_____

_____

_____

_____

_____

_____

_____

_____

_____

_____

_____

_____

_____

_____

_____

_____

_____

_____

Today's Date_____

My Thoughts

_____
_____
_____
_____
_____
_____
_____
_____
_____
_____
_____
_____
_____
_____
_____
_____
_____
_____
_____
_____
_____
_____
_____
_____

CHAPTER EIGHT

Prayer Promises

TO REMEMBER

Partakers of His Nature

We know that through the new birth we are indwelt by the Holy Spirit. The Holy Spirit is His divine nature. Think about that! Scripture says we are partakers of His divine nature! His divine power has given to us all things that pertain to life and godliness, through the knowledge of Him who called us by glory and virtue, by which have been given to us exceedingly great and precious promises, that through these you may be partakers of the divine nature, having escaped the corruption that is in the world through lust. (2 Peter 1:3–4)

Abide in God

If you abide in Me, and My words abide in you, you will ask what you desire, and it shall be done for you. John 15:7 This Book of the Law shall not depart from your mouth, but you shall meditate in it day and night, that you may observe to do according to all that is written in it. For then you will make your way prosperous, and then you will have good success. (Joshua 1:8)

[We] thank God without ceasing, because when you received the word of God which you heard from us, you welcomed it not as the word of men, but as it is in truth, the word of God, which also effectively works in you who believe. (1 Thessalonians 2:13)

God Is Powerful
It is the Spirit who gives life; the flesh profits nothing. The words that I speak to you are spirit, and they are life. (John 6:63)

So shall My Word be that goes forth from My mouth; it shall not return to Me void, but it shall accomplish what I please, and it shall prosper in the thing for which I sent it. (Isaiah 55:11)

And what is the exceeding greatness of His power toward us who believe, according to the working of His mighty power which He worked in Christ when He raised Him from the dead... (Ephesians 1:19–20)

We are His workmanship, created in Christ Jesus for good works, which God prepared beforehand that we should walk in them. (Ephesians 2:10)

In Time of Trouble
He who has begun a good work in you will complete it until the day of Jesus Christ. (Philippians 1:6)

The Lord will deliver me from every evil work and pre-serve me for His heavenly kingdom. To Him be glory forever and ever. Amen! (2 Timothy 4:18)

For Protection

No evil shall befall you, nor shall any plague come near your dwelling; for He shall give His angels charge over you, to keep you in all your ways. (Psalm 91:10–1)

Promises for Answered Prayer

Be anxious for nothing, but in everything by prayer and supplication, with thanksgiving, let your requests be made known to God; and the peace of God, which sur-passes all understanding, will guard your hearts and minds through Christ Jesus. (Philippians 4:6–7)

Whatever you ask in My name, that I will do, that the Father may be glorified in the Son. If you ask anything in My name, I will do it. (John 14:13–14)

Most assuredly, I say to you, whatever you ask the Father in My name He will give you. Until now you have asked nothing in My name. Ask, and you will receive, that your joy may be full. (John 16:23–24)

All the promises of God in Him are Yes, and in Him Amen, to the glory of God through us. (2 Corinthians 1:2)

Now to Him who is able to do exceedingly abundantly above all that we ask or think, according to the power that works in us, to Him be glory in the church by Christ Jesus to all generations, forever and ever. Amen. (Ephesians 3:20–21)

My God shall supply all your need according to His riches in glory by Christ Jesus. (Philippians 4:19)

This is the confidence that we have in Him, that if we ask anything according to His will, He hears us. And if we know that He hears us, whatever we ask, we know that we have the petitions that we have asked of Him. 1 (John 5:14–15)

Jesus's Words: Forgiveness; Prayer

When you pray, you shall not be like the hypocrites. For they love to pray standing in the synagogues and on the corners of the streets, that they may be seen by men. Assuredly, I say to you, they have their reward. But you, when you pray, go into your room, and when you have shut your door, pray to your Father who is in the secret place; and your Father who sees in secret will reward you openly. And when you pray, do not use vain repetitions as the heathen do. For they think that they will be heard for their many words. Therefore do not be like them. For your Father knows the things you have need of before you ask Him. In this manner, therefore, pray:

Our Father in heaven,
Hallowed be Your name.
Your kingdom come.
Your will be done
On earth as it is in heaven.
Give us this day our daily bread.
And forgive us our debts,
As we forgive our debtors.

And do not lead us into temptation,
But deliver us from the evil one.
For Yours is the kingdom and the power
and the glory forever. Amen.
For if you forgive men their trespasses,
your heavenly Father will also forgive you.
But if you do not forgive men their trespasses,
neither will your Father forgive your trespasses.
(Matthew 6:5–15)

Today's Date_____

My Prayers

_____

_____

_____

_____

_____

_____

_____

_____

_____

_____

_____

_____

_____

_____

_____

_____

_____

_____

_____

_____

_____

_____

_____

_____

Today's Date_____

My Answers

_____

_____

_____

_____

_____

_____

_____

_____

_____

_____

_____

_____

_____

_____

_____

_____

_____

_____

_____

_____

_____

_____

*Today's Date*_____

My Thoughts

_____
_____
_____
_____
_____
_____
_____
_____
_____
_____
_____
_____
_____
_____
_____
_____
_____
_____
_____
_____
_____
_____
_____
_____
_____

CHAPTER NINE

Research

ON FORGIVENESS

These research projects study the effects of forgiveness on stress, happiness, coping with major illness, and more.

"Interpersonal Forgiveness: The Role of Cognitive Appraisal, Empathy & Humility"

Peter Hill, Ph.D., in the Department of Psychology at Grove City College, at the time of funding, and now at Biola University, Rosemead School of Psychology, will investigate an individual's right to decide to forgive or not to forgive (or seek forgiveness). The study consists of using a survey, interviews, and workshops to help evaluate the measures of stress reduction. The objectives include understanding how different people have differing perceptions of wrongdoing, experiencing empathy towards the other person, and being more able to request and offer forgiveness.

"Psychosocial Effects of Forgiveness Training with Adults"
Carl Thoresen, Ph.D., professor of psychology at Stanford University, will study methods of helping people forgive in order to reduce hostility and anger toward their offenders. Thoresen believes that people who replace anger, hostility, and hatred with forgiveness will have better cardiovascular health and fewer long-term health problems. This project uses assessments, interviews, and group sessions. The study will incorporate men and women as a means to study if gender differences exist in forgiveness and if so, to clarify those differences. Thoresen's project was directed by Dr. Fred Luskin.

Mayo Clinic:
Forgiveness: Letting go of grudges and bitterness
When someone you care about hurts you, you can hold on to anger, resentment and thoughts of revenge — or embrace forgiveness and move forward.

http://www.mayoclinic.com/health/forgiveness/mh00131

Here, Katherine Piderman, Ph.D., staff chaplain at Mayo Clinic, Rochester, Minn., discusses forgiveness and how it can lead you down the path of physical, emotional and spiritual well-being.

Forgiveness in Health Research and Medical Practice:
http://www.explorejournal.com/article/S15508307%2805%2900154-0/abstract

Everett L. Worthington Jr, PhD1; Charlotte vanOyen Witvliet, PhD2; Andrea J. Lerner, BS1; Michael Scherer, MS1:

In this issue, Worthington, Witvliet, Lerner, and Scherer discuss how forgiveness is taking its place as an important issue in healthcare.

Many readers of EXPLORE may not realize that "forgiveness research" even exists. The field is indeed new, but, over the past decade, it has grown exponentially and is maturing admirably. We now know that there is not just a psychology underlying forgiveness but a physiology as well.

Forgiveness is an ancient concept. It is enshrined in all the great religions as a gesture of supreme value. It is a mark of compassion, love, and caring—and is thus a natural concern of the healing professions, whose essence embodies these very qualities.

There are no boundaries to forgiveness. Although Worthington et al focus on the importance of forgiveness within and between individuals, forgiveness is also being discussed at national and international levels. Should creditor nations forgive third-world debt? Should those who have been enslaved forgive their oppressors? Should victims of holocausts forgive their tormentors? Can we summon the humility that is required to seek forgiveness for our attempted genocide of native peoples? For degrading our environment, the only home we have?

A society that cannot forgive is one without a heart. We should not wish to live in such a society—or a world—in which forgiveness is never extended. With the escalating religious and political hatreds around the world, and the increasingly sinister ways of seeking vengeance, it is uncertain whether a civilization that is devoid of forgiveness can continue to exist.

These considerations exceed the concerns of Worthington et al, but they follow naturally from their findings. These authors and the forgiveness researchers they cite are onto something exceedingly important, something that is essential not just to our welfare but to our survival as well.

—Larry Dossey, MD
Executive Editor, EXPLORE

Freeing Myself Through Forgiveness
by Yolanda Young
http://www.npr.org/templates/story/story.php?storyId=14547176&ps=rs

Yolanda Young is a lawyer in Washington, D.C., and author of the book and syndicated column, "On Our Way to Beautiful." She previously worked for the National Football League Players' Association. Young is on the board of the PEN/Faulkner Foundation.

Stanford Medical University Study

Stanford Medicine, Volume 16, Number 4, Summer 1999, which is published quarterly by Stanford University Medical Center:

The Art and Science of Forgiveness

If you feel good but want to feel even better, try forgiving someone. —FREDERIC LUSKIN, PH.D.

For centuries, the world's religious and spiritual traditions have recommended the use of forgiveness as a balm for hurt or angry feelings. Psychotherapists have worked to help their clients to forgive, and some have written about the importance of forgiveness. Until recently, however, the scientific

literature has not had much to say about the effect of forgiveness. But that's starting to change. While the scientific study of forgiveness is just beginning—the relevant intervention research having been conducted only during the past ten years—when taken together, the work so far demonstrates the power of forgiveness to heal emotional wounds and hints that forgiveness may play a role in physical healing as well. What is intriguing about this research is that even people who are not depressed or particularly anxious can obtain the improved emotional and psychological functioning that comes from learning to forgive. This suggests that forgiveness may enable people whos are functioning adequately to feel even better. Published studies on forgiveness have shown the importance of forgiveness training on coping with a variety of psychologically painful experiences.

Studies have been conducted with adolescents who felt neglected by their parents, with women who were abused as children, with elderly women who felt hurt or uncared for, with males who disagreed with their female partners' decisions to have abortions and with college students who had been hurt.

These studies showed that when given forgiveness training of varying lengths and intensities, participants could become less hurt and become more able to forgive their offenders.

Forgiveness heals the heart, research hints
May 20, 1999: Web posted at: 4:00 p.m. EDT (2000 GMT)

From Medical Correspondent Eileen O'Connor

WASHINGTON (CNN) -- Littleton. Kosovo. Now Georgia. Never before, say some experts, has there been such a need to forgive what seems to be the unforgivable.

Studies funded by the Templeton Forgiveness Research Campaign are trying to monitor and measure the physiological effects of forgiveness and its benefits, taken from the pulpit into the lab.

Everett Worthington is the director of the campaign. One day after mailing off his manuscript outlining a step-by-step process of forgiveness, his own ability was sorely tested when his mother was murdered.

http://www.cnn.com/HEALTH/9905/20/forgiveness/

CHAPTER TEN

My Prayer

JOURNAL

This section has been added, just so you can have a bit more space to keep your prayers, answers, and thoughts.

Things to Remember

1. God *can* do a new thing. He is not limited.

2. He is there for you.

3. God loves you. Your relationship with God is your greatest gift. Nurture it. It will grow.

4. All you are and can be comes from your life in Jesus Christ. Draw near to Him.

    Walk with Him. Talk with Him. Philippians 4:19 says that God will provide all of your needs according to His riches in glory by Christ Jesus.

Today's Date_____

My Prayers

_____
_____
_____
_____
_____
_____
_____
_____
_____
_____
_____
_____
_____
_____
_____
_____
_____
_____
_____
_____
_____
_____
_____
_____
_____
_____

Today's Date_____

My Answers

_____
_____
_____
_____
_____
_____
_____
_____
_____
_____
_____
_____
_____
_____
_____
_____
_____
_____
_____
_____
_____
_____
_____

*Today's Date*_____

My Thoughts

_____
_____
_____
_____
_____
_____
_____
_____
_____
_____
_____
_____
_____
_____
_____
_____
_____
_____
_____
_____
_____
_____
_____
_____

*Today's Date*_____

My Prayers

_____
_____
_____
_____
_____
_____
_____
_____
_____
_____
_____
_____
_____
_____
_____
_____
_____
_____
_____
_____
_____
_____
_____
_____

Today's Date_____

My Answers

_____
_____
_____
_____
_____
_____
_____
_____
_____
_____
_____
_____
_____
_____
_____
_____
_____
_____
_____
_____
_____
_____
_____

*Today's Date*_____

My Thoughts

_____
_____
_____
_____
_____
_____
_____
_____
_____
_____
_____
_____
_____
_____
_____
_____
_____
_____
_____
_____
_____
_____
_____
_____
_____
_____
_____

Today's Date_____

My Prayers

_____
_____
_____
_____
_____
_____
_____
_____
_____
_____
_____
_____
_____
_____
_____
_____
_____
_____
_____
_____
_____
_____
_____
_____

*Today's Date*_____

My Answers

_____
_____
_____
_____
_____
_____
_____
_____
_____
_____
_____
_____
_____
_____
_____
_____
_____
_____
_____
_____
_____
_____
_____
_____